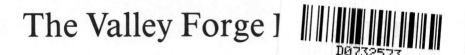
The Valley Forge

EPIC ON THE SCHUYLKILL

By John B. B. Trussell, Jr.

Commonwealth of Pennsylvania
PENNSYLVANIA HISTORICAL
AND MUSEUM COMMISSION
Harrisburg, 1989

First Printing, 1974

EPIC ON THE SCHUYLKILL

PROLOGUE

V alley Forge is not the site of a great battle, but it has long been recognized as the site of a great victory—a victory of the human spirit. It was a triumph of endurance and dedication over starvation, nakedness, cold, disease, and uncertainty. In addition, it marks the transition of a determined but disparate, untrained, and independent-minded band of men into an effective, disciplined fighting force.

For generations of Americans, Valley Forge has provided a symbol of patriotic devotion, epitomizing the ideals which brought our nation into being and which have determined its character throughout the succeeding years. The pages which follow seek to convey some idea of what the experience was like for the men who endured and, in the end, surmounted it.

VALLEY FORGE: THE PLACE

The area where the American army spent the winter of 1777-78 comprises a rough triangle of some two thousand acres. Bounded on the north for nearly three miles by the Schuylkill River, its western edge extends along Valley Creek for about a mile and a half, and its southeastern limits stretch for three and a quarter miles along a low ridge which slopes off gently toward Trout Creek on the east.

Originally, the tract containing the future encampment was part of the "Manor of Mt. Joy" which, in 1701, William Penn granted to his daughter, Letitia. About 1742, the "Mt. Joy Forge" was developed there, later coming to be known more commonly as the "Valley Forge" —not a simple blacksmith shop, but a complete ironworks. Between 1751 and 1757, a sawmill was added, and by 1757 the entire property had been purchased by John Potts, a prominent Quaker ironmaster. In 1758 or 1759, he erected a gristmill. About 1774, one of John Potts's sons, Isaac, built a stone house on the eastern side of Valley Creek near the Schuylkill. A larger house was built nearby and within a short time, William Dewees, a son-in-law of John Potts, had acquired this house and, along with Isaac Potts, joint ownership of the forge.

1

Before the British Came: The Mt. Joy Iron Works, or Valley Forge.

The coming of war in 1775 gave the Mt. Joy establishment signifi-cance as a source of military materials, and a large part of the output was devoted to the war effort. It was thus a logical military objective when fighting moved to Pennsylvania. British forces reached Valley Forge on September 18, 1777, and before leaving on September 23, they burned the sawmill and the forge, although the gristmill was spared.

THE PRELIMINARIES

Early in September, 1777, a British army under Sir William Howe landed at the northern end of Chesapeake Bay, aiming to occupy Phila-delphia, the American capital. George Washington interposed his American army between the British and the city. The two forces clashed indecisively at Brandywine Creek, then Howe sideslipped northwestward. Although Washington tried to block the advance, he was outmaneuvered and, on September 23, the British crossed the Schuylkill near Valley Forge, moving between Washington and Phila-delphia. An American attack on the British at Germantown on October 4 was beaten off. The British moved into winter quarters in the city, and after hovering in the offing until mid-December, doing what he could to threaten the invading force, Washington moved to Gulph Mills, on his way to Valley Forge, which had been selected for the American army's winter encampment.

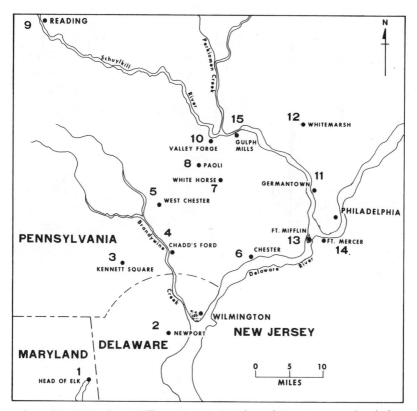

Aug. 28, 1777, Gen. William Howe's British and Hessian army landed at Head of Elk, Md. (1), to begin an advance on Philadelphia. George Washington's American army took up a blocking position near Newport, Del. (2). Sept. 9, Howe side-slipped to Kennett Square (3); Americans deployed at Chadd's Ford (4), but were defeated there in the Battle of the Brandywine, Sept. 11. While Howe continued northward via West Chester (5), Americans reassembled at Chester (6), then marched northwest to intercept Howe near White Horse (7), but heavy rain prevented a battle. Leaving Anthony Wayne's division near Paoli (8), Washington crossed the Schuylkill to protect his major supply depot at Reading (9) against possible attack. Sept. 20, British troops surprised Wayne at Paoli, moving on to occupy and burn Valley Forge (10). Feinting toward Reading to cause Washington to leave downstream fords uncovered, Howe crossed the Schuylkill, moving Sept. 25 to defensive positions at Germantown (11) and sending a detachment to occupy Philadelphia. Oct. 4, Washington's attack on Germantown was beaten off. Howe moved into Philadelphia, and Washington occupied a line of hills at Whitemarsh (12). Howe then struck at Forts Mifflin (13) and Mercer (14), which were blocking the Delaware. Fort Mifflin was abandoned Nov. 15, Fort Mercer Nov. 20. On Dec. 5, Howe moved against Whitemarsh, but fell back to Philadelphia Dec. 9. On Dec. 11, Washington left Whitemarsh, crossing the Schuylkill near Gulph Mills (15), where the army camped until Dec. 19, when it went into winter quarters at Valley Forge.

The campaign had been exhausting. The army was almost starving. During the warm days of early fall, many men had lost or improvidently thrown away their blankets. The marching and counter-marching had been hard on clothing—more than two thousand men were barefoot. Many were sick. Private Elijah Fisher noted in his diary that "We had no tents nor anything to Cook our provisions in and that was Prity Poor for beef was very leen and no salt nor any way to Cook it but throw it on the Coles and brile it and the warter we had to Drink and mix our flower with was out of a brook that run along by the Camps and so many a dippin and washin it which maid it very Dirty and muddy."

Hopefully, the situation could be improved in winter quarters. About eighteen miles from Philadelphia, Valley Forge was too remote for surprise British raids, yet close enough for the Americans to interfere with foraging parties from the city. The ground offered good defensive possibilities, and the surrounding farmlands might provide food and forage.

Accordingly, on December 19, Washington put his troops in motion. The sick were sent to Reading, and at 10 A.M. the remaining eleven thousand men started for Valley Forge, about six miles away. The road was frozen into rough ruts that were hard enough on shoes; for the soldiers who were barefoot, every step must have been agony. A cutting wind blasted a fine, light snow. Nevertheless, the last of the men reached the new campsite by nightfall, less than seven hours after the leading elements had started. Under good conditions, eleven thousand men in Indian file (the only formation the soldiers yet knew) would need upwards of six hours to complete such a move. Considering the weather, the road, and the men's condition, their performance is impressive.

Initial Arrangements at Valley Forge

No advance party was sent ahead to guide the regiments to designated bivouac areas. With night falling, there was considerable confusion. Finally, tents were pitched, but many men, having no blankets, huddled beside fires all night. There was almost nothing to eat; for some, nothing to drink. Private Joseph Martin asked two men with full canteens for water; they refused to give him any but finally sold him a "draught" for three pence in Pennsylvania currency—all the money he had.

Starvation was an imminent possibility. On December 21, what looked like an incipient mutiny developed as the chant spread through camp, "No meat, no meat." Further, when British foragers were reported and Washington ordered a force to be assembled to attack them, he learned that there was not enough food to provision even a small field force. The army's resources were only twenty-five barrels of flour; there were no animals that could be butchered, and no prospects of new supplies. Desperately, Washington wrote that "unless some great and capital change suddenly takes place . . . this Army must inevitably . . . starve, dissolve or disperse. . . ."

Exposure was an equal threat. On December 20, orders directed that the division commanders "accompanied by the Ingenieurs are to view the Ground attentively and fix upon the proper spott for hutting. . . ." The snow had ceased on the nineteenth but the weather remained cold. By December 23, lack of shoes or clothing had made 2,898 men unfit for duty. With no time to lose, those who were able began energetically to build shelters. Tom Paine, visiting the camp, wrote that "They appeared to me like a family of beavers."

On Christmas Day there was no rum to issue the gill of spirits with which Washington habitually noted special occasions. Washington himself invited the Marquis de Lafayette and the various Officers of the Day to dine with him, but could serve only small portions of veal, mutton, potatoes, and cabbage, with nothing but water to drink. Furthermore, that day brought a heavy snow which continued through the night to accumulate some four inches.

Washington, having promised the soldiers to "share in the Hardships and partake of every inconvenience," had been living in a tent, warmed only from a fire outside. Now he found it impossible to handle his responsibilities without better shelter. Like many of the other generals, he sought housing in a local residence: for £100 in Pennsylvania currency he rented Isaac Potts's house from its current tenant, the twice-widowed Mrs. Deborah Hewes, whose first husband had been one of Isaac's brothers.

The weather continued very cold. Three days after Christmas there was another four-inch snow, with temperatures dropping even lower, and still more snow on the twenty-ninth. By December 30, the Schuylkill had frozen and the snow was half a foot deep. But shelters had been begun. Rations, although irregular in arrival and inadequate in quantity, had continued to come in. At New Year's, it was possible to issue each man a gill of rum. As Dr. Albigence Waldo wrote in his journal, "We got some Spirits and finish'd the Year with a good Drink & thankfull hearts in our new Hutt."

The Huts

By no means all troops were in "hutts" by December 31, but substantial beginnings had been made.

Before leaving Gulph Mills, Washington directed the formation of twelve-man squads, each to build its own hut, to be made of logs chinked with clay, six and a half feet high, fourteen feet wide, and sixteen feet long, with a fireplace in the rear, made of wood and "secured" with clay. They were to be aligned along company streets, doors facing the street. Behind the enlisted men's huts was to be a line of identical huts for officers; but instead of twelve men, each would house the officers of two companies, the field officers (major through colonel) of a regiment, the members of a brigade staff, or one general officer.

Roofing was left to individual ingenuity, and Washington offered a $100 reward for the best suggestion for a substitute for board roofs.

Private Joseph Clark's squad roofed its hut with leaves—presumably evergreen branches, as the deciduous trees would have long been bare. The quartermasters were ordered to procure "large quantities" of straw for roofing and bedding; if the local farmers objected to providing straw on grounds that the wheat had not yet been threshed,

Drawing by H. T. McNeill, courtesy Stephen Moylan Press.

Replica of Soldiers' Hut, Valley Forge.

"the Straw will be taken with the Grain in it and paid for as Straw only." Some huts were roofed with tent canvas—an unauthorized practice which was promptly forbidden. In other cases, saplings were used, or earth covered with splints.

Timber, although green, was plentiful. Tools and nails, however, were extremely scarce. Draft animals were few, starved, and weak, so the men dragged the logs they cut through the frozen mud to the building sites.

Half-trained and highly individualistic, the troops paid little attention to the prescribed pattern. To use fewer logs or to reduce the area exposed to wind, many dug their floors almost two feet below ground level. Whatever its advantages, this practice contributed to dampness and general unhealthfulness. Hut areas excavated during archeological projects have also revealed wide diversity in lateral dimensions, many being substantially smaller than the prescribed size, one being only eight by ten feet. Another variation is that, of the hut areas studied, one had its fireplace on the side; in several others the fireplace was on one of the rear corners; and in the huts with fireplaces in the rear, some were flush with the wall and others were recessed into alcoves.

Uniformity was less urgent than speed. Washington offered a twelve-dollar prize for the first well-constructed hut completed in each regiment, and by nightfall of December 21, one structure was finished. By December 29, some nine hundred huts were under construction, but it was February 8 before Washington reported that "most of the men are now in tolerable good Hutts."

"Tolerable" was the key word. There was no ventilation except through the doors—where windows existed, they were covered with oiled paper, and not until May 14 were orders issued for each hut to have two windows. Because chimneys were poorly constructed, or because the firewood was green, many huts were filled with smoke. On the other hand, Dr. Waldo commented, "We have got our Hutts to be very comfortable, and feel ourselves happy in them."

One problem was filth. On January 7, Officers of the Day were ordered to check each hut's interior morning and evening for cleanliness. But archeological excavations show that bones from meat that had been eaten were simply tossed into corners. Apart from the menace to health, the combination of decaying animal matter with the crowding together of unwashed men clad in filthy rags must have been extremely noxious. As late as May 27, an order stated that the chinking of the huts was to be removed "and every other method taken to render them as airy as possible."

7

Archeological studies indicate the possibility that poles were anchored in small holes in the floors to support bunks or other furniture. Straw, when obtainable, provided mattresses. Each squad was allotted one pail, subject to availability. Lafayette described the huts as "little shanties that are scarcely gayer than dungeon cells." Their inadequacies were certainly a factor in the army's high disease and death rates, but malnutrition, insufficient clothing, and wretched hygiene would undoubtedly have taken a heavy toll by themselves.

SHORTAGES

The prescribed ration was a pound of bread, a pound of either meat or stockfish, a pint of milk, a quart of beer, peas, beans, and butter. In practice, the stated ration was meaningless, the reality being the bare subsistence level that could be maintained by the army's own efforts.

Foraging detachments were sent into the countryside, but meat continued to be extremely limited. On the first two days of 1778, there was none at all. On January 5, Washington wrote that even with "the most sparing œconomy" the meat supplies would not last more than two days. Some must have come in, though, for on January 13 Washington officially condemned butchers who had "extorted money from the soldiers" for the "plucks" of the beef—i.e., hearts, livers, and lights. But on January 28, the available resources in cattle amounted only to ninety head. On February 11, some brigades had received no issues of beef for four days; and on February 15, some units had gone even longer. On February 26, General Nathanael Greene stated that he and other officers had taken up a collection which provided temporary relief. Clearly, some foodstuffs must have been available for local purchase. The problem was in official procurement.

With March, the situation began to ease. An order of March 15 implies that cattle were being slaughtered on a daily basis. Late in the month, a herd of approximately five hundred cattle was expected. Conditions improved in April. The annual shad run in the Schuylkill brought a massive netting of fish. The ration was fixed at a pound and a half of flour or bread, a pound of beef or fish or three-quarters of a pound of pork, and a gill of spirits; or a pound and a half of pork or bacon, half a pint of peas or beans, and one gill of spirits. On April 19, Washington was concerned that only well-fattened stock be sent to Valley Forge.

Shortages of bread had been equally drastic. Ovens were soon built in the basement of the Dewees House, which was referred to as the

8

"Bakehouse" as early as January 4. But flour supplies were uncertain, and for six consecutive days during February none was received. Rice was ordered for the sick, but "Indian meal" had to be authorized as a substitute. When other supplies failed, the troops were usually able to collect enough flour for "firecake," a concoction of flour and water baked on a griddle.

Drawing by H. T. McNeill, courtesy Stephen Moylan Press.
William Dewees' Residence—The "Bakehouse."

Procurement of spirits was another problem which, because of the place of liquor in the eighteenth-century diet, was serious. On January 1, Nathanael Greene reported the "murmurs" of his officers, and suggested that stocks be requisitioned from known locations and allocated at the rate of thirty or forty gallons for the officers of each regiment. "This," he concluded, "would give a temporary relief. . . ." Perhaps in response, Washington authorized the commissary to sell the officers, on credit, "small proportionable quantities of Spirits." On January 26, prices were fixed for various types of liquor. Whiskey was to cost six shillings a quart. On April 16, the price was lowered to four shillings.

Shortage of forage created equal hardship for the army's horses. Before Christmas Washington transferred the Light Horse unit under the Polish Count Casimir Pulaski to Trenton, New Jersey, and on January 6 prohibited retention of all "private horses." Even so, on

February 12 the congressional Committee on Conference investigating conditions at Valley Forge warned that if the British should attack, the American cannon would probably be captured simply for lack of horses to move them. Two weeks later, the artillery commander, General Henry Knox, wrote that hundreds of horses had starved to death. April brought improvement in the ability to provide for the surviving horses, and the end of the month saw the first arrivals of remounts, with more coming in about mid-May. By May 24, it was possible to return cavalry units to Valley Forge. All told, though, it is estimated that no fewer than fifteen hundred horses had died.

As for clothing, long marches had worn out shoes and reduced clothes to rags. At Valley Forge, the damp weather rotted fabrics, and the frozen ruts covering large parts of the campsite shredded shoe-leather. "Few men have more than one Shirt," Washington wrote on December 23, "many only the Moiety of one, and Some none at all." During the next week he listed pressing needs for shoes, stockings, and blankets.

One expedient was to barter for shoes the hides of cattle slaughtered for food, at four pence per pound for hides and ten shillings a pair for shoes. Eventually, this proved very effective; however, given the months-long shortage of cattle and considering that, at these rates, one pair of shoes cost thirty pounds of rawhide and that more than two thousand men were already barefoot, this program obviously could not have provided a rapid solution.

On January 1, each regiment was directed to report the number of its "taylors," who were excused from other duties "to be imploy'd in making up the Cloaths for their respective Reg^{ts}." Perhaps there was no connection, but on January 4, Washington announced that he was "pained" to learn that "Some Tents have already been cut up by the Soldiers and disposed off," presumably for clothing.

Parties were sent out to seize clothing from civilians. Admitting that this caused "the greatest alarm and uneasiness," Washington stated flatly that "The alternative was to dissolve the Army." On December 29, Washington sent letters to the state governments, pleading for clothing. On January 6, requests for donations of clothes for the sick were broadcast through the churches.

A ray of light came about January 1, when General William Smallwood, commanding at Wilmington, Delaware, reported the capture of the British brig, *Symmetry*. Among her other cargo was "Scarlet, Blue, & Buff Cloth, sufficient to Cloath all the Officers of the Army, & Hats, Shirts, Stockings, Shoes, Boots, Spurs, &c. to finish compleat Suits for all." But conditions over-all remained appalling. When some Virginians' enlistments expired, orders required them to turn in their blankets. This must have caused complaint, as a brigade order two days later offered a conciliatory explanation. "The distress for Blankets," it said, "makes it necessary to retain those the Soldiers have who is then discharged. This the Brigadier hopes will be readily complyed with By the men who are going home in order to afford more Comfort to their Brother Soldiers who keep the Field." Sentries stood on their hats to shield their feet from the icy ground. The sick, helpless to protest, were robbed of their clothes. Many of the dead were buried naked, stripped to provide for survivors. Since numerous deaths were from contagious diseases, this helped spread infection. As of February 5, there were 3,989 men who, lacking clothes or shoes, were unavailable for duty. Soon after the middle of February, Lafayette wrote that "The unfortunate soldiers are in want of everything; they have neither coats, hats, shirts or shoes." About this time, a newly arrived foreign volunteer who called himself Friedrich von Steuben was inspecting the troops with a professional military eye. Later, he wrote that

> The men were literally naked. . . . The officers who had coats had them of every color and make. I saw officers at a grand parade at Valley Forge mounting guard in a sort of dressing gown made of an old blanket or woolen bed cover.

By March, supplies began to arrive from France, although on March 6 Washington complained of French shoes "affording little more than a day's wear." The next day he reported that some cloth had come in from Virginia. However, the supply of blankets continued to be less than adequate. As the month passed, the situation improved. Indeed, troops were accused of selling their clothes to buy liquor, and show-down inspections were ordered. More supplies arrived from France, but as late as May 21 some men lacked shirts, and no reserves were available. On June 18—just before the army's final departure— upwards of a hundred men were still unable to march due to lack of shoes. This was a far cry from the two thousand barefoot soldiers who had stumbled into camp in December, but it shows that clothing shortages at Valley Forge were never completely eliminated.

Requirements were reported to the responsible authorities by Washington and the Committee on Conference, but no one sat waiting for shortages to be supplied.

At the very beginning, on December 22, a bridge was begun across the Schuylkill to provide access for supplies from the north. Before January ended, a rough but usable span was completed. To exploit local resources, an order of February 8 announced that a market would operate at "the Stone Chimney Pickett" on Mondays and Thursdays, at the northern end of the bridge on Tuesdays and Fridays, and near the Adjutant General's office on Wednesdays and Saturdays.

Besides permanent procurement parties in nearby areas, Washington had detachments ranging farther. In February, for example, General Anthony Wayne and five hundred men went into southern New Jersey to round up cattle. Unfortunately, many farmers hid their livestock; Wayne found only 130 head, but eighty-five of these fell into British hands and the effort of nearly a month yielded only forty-five cattle.

Bartering rawhide for shoes was mentioned. Another economy was directed in a January 12 order aimed at saving dirty tallow and ashes to make soft soap, and at "imploying proper persons to boile the Oyle out of the Cattles feet and preserve it for the use of the Army."

Although larger game had long disappeared from the area, small game animals remained, and the troops did exploit this resource. Archeological studies have identified the burned bones of squirrels, rabbits, and opossum or raccoon. The advantage taken of the shad run was mentioned. A flight of vast flocks of wild pigeons also provided, briefly, another source of food.

It appears, however, that there were limits beyond which the soldiers would not go. Under the circumstances, it might be expected that the troops would have had recourse to horsemeat. Even so, excavations have found only two horse skulls, suggesting that for whatever reason, only a few men resorted to eating horses.

The acute deficiencies did not reflect any general lack of supplies. On the contrary, within all the states, quantities of cloth were adequate and food supplies were ample. Private Martin served with a procurement squad from late December through April at Downingtown, hardly a dozen miles from camp. He stated that "We fared much better than I had ever done in the army before, or ever did afterward. We had very good provisions all winter and generally enough of them."

The congressionally-prescribed organization for supply procurement was ill-conceived, over-centralized, and inefficient. Much of the time its administration was inept or indifferent, and in some instances corrupt. The basic difficulty, however, was poor transportation.

The main supply depot at Reading was only forty miles up the Schuylkill, but until late March the river was blocked by ice or too shallow for barges. As for land movement, not only were roads few and incredibly bad, but teamsters were hard to find. Congress was willing to pay thirty shillings a day for a wagon, four horses, and a driver, but wagon contractors demanded at least forty-five shillings.

On February 15, Washington suggested that free Negroes be hired as teamsters, but the proposal does not seem to have been adopted.

Even when wagons and wagoners were obtained, miserable road conditions caused frequent breakdowns, and loads were often jettisoned. Sometimes, to reduce weight, drivers knocked in the tops of barrels of salted fish or meat and drained off the brine. Naturally, the contents spoiled; more than once, salt fish reaching Valley Forge were so rotten that they were almost liquefied.

Foraging soon exhausted supplies in the area near the camp. Dr. Waldo noted by December 22 that "The Impoverish'd Country about us, affords but little matter to employ a Thief, or keep a Clever Fellow in good humour." Food prices became inflated, and by January 20, Washington was complaining of the "avarice" of the farmers who "are endeavoring to take advantage of this Army." British gold was more appealing to many local farmers than the Continentals' debased paper currency, and numerous trials at Valley Forge convicted local citizens of attempting to sell foodstuffs to the British.

It should be pointed out that there was a general lack of awareness of the army's plight, and that this was an unavoidable result of a deliberate policy. The strong British forces only eighteen miles away had to be kept ignorant of the army's weakness. Congress and other officials were kept informed, but in concealing the facts from the enemy, any inkling of the actual situation was also kept from the country at large. Unquestionably, this prevented development of a popular sense of urgency which might have reduced some of the obstacles which contributed to the army's suffering.

MEDICINE AND HEALTH

An estimated three thousand soldiers died of disease during the winter of 1777-78. However, statistics are fragmentary, and only some thirty graves have been located. While men certainly died at Valley Forge, many of the deaths occurred at outlying hospitals.

Each regiment had a surgeon and a surgeon's mate, and a regional system operated larger, more permanent hospitals. As the sick had been sent from Gulph Mills to Reading, the men arriving at Valley Forge should all have been healthy; but within a week a number had fallen ill. Dr. Waldo stated on Christmas Day that "The poor Sick, suffer much in Tents this cold Weather." He went on to add, "But very few of the sick Men Die." However, the situation rapidly worsened. The February 12 report of the Committee on Conference noted that "The sick and dead list has increased one third in the last week's return, which was one third greater than the week preceding. . . ."

Illness continued to take its toll. As late as May 29, Washington stated that "Near 4,000 men in this Camp are sick of the small pox and other disorders." Presumably, however, those described as "sick of the small pox" were largely men suffering the after-effects of inoculation. Even so, on June 17, Washington said that there were some twenty-three hundred troops sick in camp—over eighteen per cent of his total strength of 12,500.

From the beginning, men with more serious ailments were moved into so-called "general hospitals." Besides the one at Reading, others were established at Ephrata, Bethlehem, Easton, Lititz, and Yellow Springs (modern Chester Springs). These rapidly became overcrowded. At Bethlehem, for example, between 800 and 900 patients were crammed into space intended for 360.

Medicines, blankets, even straw for bedding were lacking. Washington wrote on December 31 that "I sincerely feel for the unhappy Condition of our Poor Fellows in the Hospitals. . . . It is but too melancholy a truth, that our Hospital Stores are exceeding scanty and deficient. . . ." Shortages, combined with ignorance, led to newly admitted patients being reissued blankets or straw used by men just dead of contagious diseases; many men hospitalized with less serious illnesses thus became infected in hospital, often fatally.

Of five hundred patients entering the hospital at Bethlehem, at least one-third died. The 9th Virginia alone sent forty men to this hospital, but only one survived to return to duty. Private Fisher wrote on February 8 that "I gits better but a Number Dyed. There was between fifty and sixty Dyed in about a month."

For those not ill enough to be sent to one of the "general hospitals," orders of January 9 and January 13 directed construction of two "flying hospitals" near the center of each brigade area and not more than a hundred yards away. These were to be fifteen feet wide, twenty-five feet long, and at least nine feet high, with windows on each side and a chimney at one end. They were to be roofed only with boards or shingles; sod or dirt was forbidden. Late in January, each brigade was directed to detail a captain to visit the brigade's sick in the camp hospitals, and an order of January 15 sent two senior officers to visit the general hospitals.

The men had too few clothes to provide a change while one set was being washed, and the weather was too unpleasant to go without. Vermin and scabies inevitably spread. As early as January 8, "being . . . informed many men are rendered unfit for duty by the Itch," Washington ordered the surgeons "to look attentively into this matter

14

and as soon as the men who are affected with this disorder are properly disposed in Hutts to have them anointed for it."

Exposure and crowding made colds epidemic, and these sometimes developed into pneumonia. Unhygienic conditions contributed directly to dysentery, typhoid, and typhus. Bitter cold brought frostbite —Lafayette wrote that "feet and legs froze till they became black, and it was often necessary to amputate them."

Washington tried repeatedly to improve sanitation. On January 7, he instituted weekly fatigue parties "to cause all dead horses . . . and all Offals to be buried." He also stressed use and care of latrines ("vaults" or "necessaries," as they were called), "otherwise the Camp will be unsufferable from the Stench . . . and very prejudicial to the health." On March 13, Washington noted that despite his earlier order, "the Carcasses of Dead Horses lay in, or near the Camp, and that ye Offal . . . still lay unburied, that much Filth and nastiness, is spread amongst ye Hutts, which will soon be reduc'd to a state of putrefaction and cause a Sickly Camp." He went on to say that "Out of tender regard for ye lives & health of his brave Soldiery, . . . He again in ye most positive terms, orders & Commands" that the dead horses be buried, and that old vaults be filled and new ones dug.

On April 14, Washington praised the neatness of some areas; but in many, he added, "the case was otherwise; and . . . the smell of some places intollerable. . . ." Therefore, for "any Soldier who shall attempt to ease himself any where but at a proper Necessary . . . 5 lashes are to be order'd him immediately. . . ."

The problem never was solved. By June 10, the army moved into a new area about a mile away. There, according to Captain John Laurens, "We shall not swallow the effluvia arising from a deposit of . . . filth accumulated during six months."

The increasing clothing supply and the onset of warm weather permitted better personal cleanliness. On May 14, troops were excused from further Friday afternoon duties to launder clothing, and sergeants were to march their squads to bathe in the river; to avoid the risk of chills, however, they were warned "to be careful that no man remains longer than ten minutes in the water."

Smallpox was an ever-present threat. Although a crude form of immunization was known, few recruits had been inoculated. Further, there was little opportunity to immunize troops during a campaign. The winter encampment offered a chance to complete inoculations for the army at large: on January 6, surgeons were instructed to report men who had never had smallpox, and an immunization program began. Private Fisher reported on February 28 that "I was anockulated for the Small poxe and had it Prity favorable to what others had it." But supplies were inadequate to care for everyone who would be made sick by inoculation; consequently, the program had to be phased over a period of time, prolonging the chances of an epidemic.

Most medical officers appear to have been capable and conscientious. The same is not true, in general, of the hospital orderlies. The work was unpleasant and the risk of infection high, so the more undesirable and irresponsible men tended to be detailed to hospital duty. Predictably, many patients received care which was indifferent or—as in the case of the reuse of the straw and blankets of men just dead of typhus—fatally harmful. In sharp contrast is the devoted service volunteered by members of the religious communities at Ephrata and Lititz, many of whom became infected, quite a number fatally. Significant use of women nurses in military hospitals still lay decades in the future, although on May 31, Washington did urge employment as nurses of as many "Women of the Army" as could be recruited. Probably, his aim was to free soldiers for field service, for he went on to specify that "Orderlies are to be appointed of those who want of Cloathing, lameness, &c, and are unfit to march."

During the Valley Forge winter, the authorities did the best they knew. In light of medical science of the time and within the constraints of the situation, the results that developed had to be expected.

PROVISIONS FOR DEFENSE

An important factor in choosing Valley Forge for an encampment was its defensibility. In the basic layout, brigade hut areas were allocated in terms of assigned tactical sectors. While initial efforts went into constructing huts and completing the bridge, by January 15 Washington was urging that "The works mark'd out by the Ingenieurs for the defence of the Camp are to be executed with all possible dispatch."

Tactically, the critical terrain was a ridge running north and then northeast from Mt. Joy. The Valley Creek gorge made the position unassailable from the west. The northern flank was given some security by the river, although the shallow water and the new bridge were potential weaknesses. However, the best avenues of approach for an attacking force were through the open country to the southeast and along the three roads which penetrated the area: one near the river (approximating the course of the modern Port Kennedy road); a second, farther south, leading to Gulph Mills; and a third (Baptist Road) running south from the eastern slopes of Mt. Joy ridge.

16

The main line of resistance was established along the forward slope of Mt. Joy ridge, above Baptist Road, to the bluffs above the Schuylkill. It consisted of a continuous ditch, some six feet wide but only three or four feet deep, not for cover but for a dry moat against an attacker; cover was provided by a mound of earth behind the ditch. At this line's southern end, dug-in artillery emplacements and an earthen redoubt, called Fort Washington, covered the entrance of Baptist Road into the camp. At the northern end, where the Port Kennedy road crossed, was another artillery emplacement, together with a second earthen fort, called Fort Huntington. About four hundred yards to the front of the ditch was a line of abatis—sharpened stakes angling forward, comparable to a barbed-wire entanglement. Covering this was another gun emplacement, at the northern end. The whole complex was known as the inner-line defense.

The outpost line of resistance, or "outer line," consisted of entrenchments from Baptist Road northeastward almost to the Port Kennedy road, along the ridge forming the hypotenuse of the right triangle enclosing the encampment. At its northern end were two more earthworks, Fort John Moore and Fort Mordecai Moore (now called **Fort Greene** and **Fort Muhlenberg**), flanking the Port Kennedy road.

On the bluff above the bridge was a star-shaped fort. The northern approach to the bridge was also guarded by a detachment posted across the Schuylkill. Other pickets were deployed well beyond the camp toward Philadelphia on both sides of the river.

The works were never fully completed, but the project was pursued as weather and competing requirements permitted. On January 20, Washington directed the officers "to Exert themselves to put the **Camp** in a[s] defenceless [sic] a Condition as possible," and all off-duty soldiers of brigades in the outer-line sector were to fall out every morning at 9 A.M. to work on the entrenchments. But as late as March 27, the main line of resistance was still unfinished, and Washington urged brigade commanders to get the defenses completed. Apparently, this appeal spurred excessive zeal, for less than a week later, an order stated that "As the Stumps and Brush in front of the new line afford an excellent obstacle to the approach of an enemy, 'tis expressly forbid, that any of it should be burnt . . . for the distance of extreme Musketrange in front of the line." By April 26, the fortifications were about as fully completed as they were to be, with the trenches and abatis along the main line of resistance and the emplacements and redoubts at its flanks being finished and manned.

Fifteen infantry brigades were deployed. From south to north along the main line of resistance were three brigades—William Maxwell's, the brigade formerly under Thomas Conway, and Lachlan McIntosh's brigade. Defense along the river was entrusted to the brigades of Jedediah Huntington and James Varnum. From west to east along the outpost line were William Woodford's and Charles Scott's brigades, Wayne's two Pennsylvania brigades, and the brigades of Enoch Poor, John Glover, Ebenezer Learned, John Paterson, George Weedon, and Peter Muhlenberg. Knox's artillery was partly located in fixed positions, but most of it was held centrally to be moved wherever needed.

Sir William Howe reported to London that the position was too strong to assault during bad weather. The coming of spring brought Howe's departure for England, and Sir Henry Clinton, his replacement, was intent on getting back to New York. Thus, the Valley Forge defenses were never tested, but they served a useful purpose. From Bunker Hill on, even raw American troops had fought well from behind cover; it seems improbable, once the position's natural advantages had been strengthened, that any attack within existing British capabilities could have dislodged Washington's force.

ORGANIZATION, TRAINING, AND WEAPONS

Another reason why the British could not drive the Americans out of Valley Forge was that, as spring progressed, Washington's troops were finally becoming a trained, disciplined, reliable fighting force.

There had of course been attempts at training, even during the autumn campaign. For example, on October 12, Washington directed that "Every day, when the weather will permit, the Corps are to be turn'd out and practic'd in . . . primeing and loading, advancing, forming, Retreating, breaking, and Rallying."

However, standards were difficult to achieve. Strengths of regiments or battalions (the terms were used interchangeably) differed from state to state, and in some cases between regiments from the same state. Furthermore, few units had ever been at anything approximating full manning, and the campaign had taken a further toll. Short-term enlistments caused rapid turn-over. Many men were detached, sometimes for months, as foragers or teamsters, or excused from duty to serve as officers' "waiters" (i.e., orderlies). As early as January 29, Washington recommended standardization of organization, but it was not until May 27, 1778, that Congress approved a standard battalion structure.

At Valley Forge, there were seventy-three infantry regiments (two of which were consolidated on January 1, 1778), plus the artillery brigade, the "corps of artificers" (engineers), and Washington's Life Guard. Total manpower as of December 23, however, was only 11,982, and as

18

Washington observed on December 27, regiments were little more than companies in size.

Through the winter, Washington pressed the states to fill their quotas. Men on detached service were recalled, and the number of servants authorized to officers was reduced. In late March, recruits began to arrive. Somewhat offsetting these gains were the losses from illness, desertion, and the expiration of enlistments.

Weapons were another problem. Given the musket's inaccuracy, effective firepower required concentrated volleys, so the weapons of any given company had to be of the same caliber and type. But the army had thirteen different kinds of muskets and a great variety of individually crafted rifles. A single company was often equipped with muskets, rifles, and fowling pieces. There was a shortage even of these, as weapons of men being discharged were seldom reclaimed. Finally, available weapons were, too often, improperly cared for, many of them rusty and some incapable of being fired.

Reloading was slow and combat occurred at close quarters, so there was seldom time for more than one or two volleys. In attack or defense, therefore, the bayonet was extremely important. Only about half of the American troops had been issued bayonets, and few had been trained to use them; General Steuben remarked disgustedly that bayonets were chiefly used as skewers to broil meat. On January 18, Washington directed that brigades having armorers were to manufacture bayonets; other brigades were to commission bayonet manufacture by civilian smiths. But on March 26, he had to repeat these instructions.

New firearms arrived irregularly. Some came from France, others were captured. But as late as May 25, at least twenty-five hundred soldiers were without muskets or awaiting return of their muskets from repair shops. Not until June 6 could Washington report that almost if not quite all troops had been equipped.

Musket replacement components had to be individually hand-wrought. The troops had hardly arrived at the winter encampment when a program was begun to repair all firearms. Every weapon was to be inspected, and any in poor condition turned in to the armorers. But as of March 6, large numbers of muskets were still under repair.

Ammunition also was short. Excess cartridges in the troops' hands were turned in, and drying and repacking of damaged cartridges became a continuing program. Repeatedly, orders were issued against wasting ammunition through improper care (compounded by the shortage of well made cartridge boxes) or unauthorized firing—an easy way of clearing a charge from the musket. As late as May 14, Washington wrote that the reserve stock of cartridges was insufficient, and on June 1, he was expressing a need for more lead.

Another major defect when the army reached Valley Forge was that the few troops who had been taught any formations and maneuvers had been trained along widely divergent lines—some on the British pattern, others on the French, and still others on the Prussian. Infantry tactics were based on close-order drill, and without a standard system, teamwork on the battlefield was almost impossible. As mentioned, the soldiers knew how to march only in Indian file. This stretched out each unit over excessive road space; completing a movement required an inordinate length of time, and straggling could not be prevented. The men did march in step, thus achieving a steadier, faster rate than by shambling along at individual gaits, but only to the beat of the drum, advertising their approach for as far as sound would carry. Even then, cadence and length of step varied from one regiment to another. Files could be deployed into line to right or left, but line to the front or rear could be formed only with confusion and delay—serious drawbacks in battle.

A particularly serious deficiency was the officers' limited concept of their duties. Influenced by British tradition, they recognized no responsibility except to lead their men in combat. Supervision of training, seeing to the men's well-being, maintenance of equipment, and insuring that directives were in fact carried out were left to the sergeants. That was acceptable in an army which, like the British, had a corps of capable non-commissioned officers, but the American army had no such corps in 1777. This misconception affected every aspect of activity; intermediate commanders tended to ignore Washington's directives—not through insubordination, but simply in ignorance that they were concerned. In sum, as Steuben observed with only slight overstatement, "With regard to their military discipline, I can safely say that no such thing existed."

An over-all supervisor of training, known then as Inspector General, already existed in the person of Thomas Conway, a European volunteer. But Washington distrusted Conway, and Conway's arrogance offended the American officers. As a result, even Conway's worthwhile proposals had been ignored, and on December 31, 1777, frustrated, he had left Valley Forge.

What was needed was a man with the professional competence to devise and carry out an effective training program and the judgment and adaptability which would lead Washington to grant him authority to administer it to all elements of the command. Such a man appeared in Friedrich von Steuben.

20

Information about him when he arrived at Valley Forge on February 23, 1778, was vague, implying that he was a lieutenant general in Frederick the Great's Prussian army. Actually, even his name was somewhat spurious. His father, a Prussian engineer officer, arbitrarily adopted the particle *von* on the strength of some distaff connections with the nobility. Friedrich himself changed the spelling of Steube to Steuben.

True, he held a Prussian commission from 1747 to 1763, but he rose no higher than captain. He served in the Seven Years War, eventually at Frederick the Great's headquarters. In 1763, Steuben left the army and became Chamberlain in the court of Hohenzollern-Hechingen, but in 1777, poverty forced the Prince of Hohenzollern-Hechingen to disband his court. Steuben, having unsuccessfully sought appointment at the court of Baden and in the armies of France, Spain, and possibly Britain, finally came to the attention of Benjamin Franklin, in Paris.

Franklin believed that Steuben had talents the American army needed, but feared that an ex-captain would get little attention. Apparently, he devised the cover story on Steuben's background, and probably briefed him on the self-seeking blunders of previous European volunteers. Certainly, he gave Steuben a letter introducing him as a lieutenant general of the Prussian army.

Steuben reported to Congress at York on February 5, 1778. Asking only for expenses, he offered to abide by whatever Congress considered his services worth, after he had demonstrated what he could do. Congress was impressed, but Washington reserved judgment. Perhaps as a test, he asked the Prussian to visit several regiments and report what remedial steps seemed necessary.

Steuben knew no English, but his military secretary, Pierre Duponceau, spoke English, and Alexander Hamilton and John Laurens of Washington's staff, both of whom spoke French, helped out. After studying the situation, Steuben drew up a training plan which Washington approved, naming Steuben as acting Inspector General.

Steuben promptly began writing a book of drill regulations. Duponceau translated it, and Hamilton and Laurens revised it into American terminology. Since March had already begun, time was short, so Steuben spent the days instructing in one phase and the evenings drawing up the next.

To demonstrate, he used Washington's forty-six-man Life Guard, arranging on March 17 for a hundred men to be added. He conducted their instruction himself, scandalizing the British-oriented American

Schematic of the Valley Forge Encampment 1777-1778

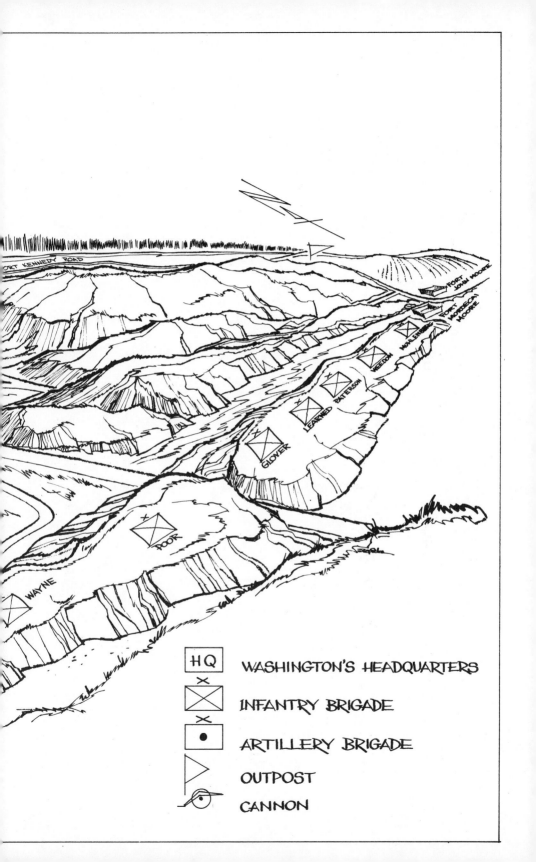

WASHINGTON'S HEADQUARTERS

INFANTRY BRIGADE

ARTILLERY BRIGADE

OUTPOST

CANNON

officers by taking a musket in his own hands to teach the manual of arms. His explosive rage at errors and his flights of profanity in a mixture of French, German, and broken English delighted the troops and he soon became popular as a "character."

He stressed simplicity, reducing the manual of arms to ten motions and reloading from nineteen to fifteen motions. He imposed a standard pace of twenty-four inches and a cadence of seventy-five steps per minute—relatively slow, but suited to rough terrain and the heavy weight of arms and ammunition—and taught the men to keep step without relying on drum-taps. He introduced platoon columns, more compact and more maneuverable, and taught the troops to wheel in line and to move quickly from column into line to front or rear. These were major improvements in battlefield effectiveness.

Uniform formation drill required uniform organizations, so Steuben was allowed to regroup units, at least provisionally, into standardized size. Effective tactical performance demanded standardized weapons, which led to reallocations to provide reasonable uniformity within any given company. Steuben's example of personal attention to details led the officers to begin to understand and carry out a vastly wider scope of responsibility. Care of equipment, individual cleanliness, and troop well-being all improved.

Conway resigned in late April, and on May 7, Washington could tell Steuben that Congress had appointed him Inspector General. It was a widely applauded move, and certainly was richly earned.

Valley Forge is correctly regarded as a monument to endurance and dedication. But Valley Forge is equally a symbol of the translation of a group of sincere but minimally trained, loosely organized, and highly individualistic men into a hard-hitting, dependable, efficient army. It would be wrong to attribute the credit exclusively or even primarily to Steuben. Many reforms were under way when he arrived, and many were outside his particular sphere of responsibility. Nevertheless, among the factors leading to the achievement realized at Valley Forge, Steuben's contributions loom large indeed.

CRIME AND PUNISHMENT

Although the army attained unprecedented levels of training and discipline at Valley Forge, numerous disciplinary problems arose, non-military as well as military.

A particularly troublesome offense was pillaging. Within a week after the army's arrival at Valley Forge, Washington was moved to a flight of outraged rhetoric, declaring that

> It is with in expressable Grief and Indignation that the General has received Information of the Cruel outrages and Robberies lately committed by Soldiers. . . . Was we in the Enemy's Country such practices would be unwarrantable, but committed against our friends are in the highest degree Base Cruel and injurious to the Cause in which we are engaged[;] they demand therefore and shall receive the severest punishment.

He went on to curtail sharply the soldiers' freedom of movement outside camp. Yet on March 3, a guard post had to be established on the south end of the Schuylkill bridge, for "notwithstanding the repeated orders . . . to prevent Soldiers from Straggling . . . the Country round about ye Camp . . . is full of them"; restrictions were tightened "to prevent ye mischiefs resulting from this pernicious practice to ye Inhabitants. . . ." But restricting men to camp did not eliminate all difficulties. On January 6 and again on April 29, William Dewees complained that troops had been stealing whatever of value remained of his burned forge.

Available records show that of 161 military personnel tried by courts martial at Valley Forge, 39 were tried for civil crimes and 122 for purely military offenses.

There were thirteen allegations of fraud, extortion, or embezzlement, eleven of assault, seven of theft, two of perjury or forgery, two of issuing challenges to duels, and one each of attempted sodomy, plundering, and manslaughter. There were six acquittals and thirty-three convictions for civil offenses, but in five of the latter Washington reduced or remitted the sentences.

The most frequent military offense was desertion, of which forty-two cases were tried. There were eighteen cases of disobedience or insubordination, sixteen of neglect of duty, fourteen of "conduct unbecoming the character of a gentleman," ten of abuse of authority, seven of absence without leave, and five each of gaming, cowardice, and violation of sundry General Orders. Convictions resulted in eighty-six cases, with sixteen of the sentences being reduced or remitted. There were twenty-six acquittals.

In addition to these cases, there were two trials of women, accused of conspiring with soldiers to mutiny and desert. One woman was convicted, the other acquitted.

Under special congressional authority, twenty-nine civilians were tried for various acts of supplying the enemy. Eight were acquitted and twenty-one convicted, but in five cases the sentences were reduced.

Under this same authority, another civilian was convicted of acting as a guide to British troops, and a second of spying.

Short of mutiny, no genuine cases of which seem to have occurred, the greatest disciplinary threat to the army's survival was desertion. The forty-two cases tried give only the barest indication of the numbers of deserters. Reliable data were seldom available even at the time: Washington complained on January 21 that, despite repeated orders for prompt reports, "it is by indirect and casual information, that this knowledge comes to the General."

Obviously, desertions occurred almost daily. On February 7, Washington wrote that "The spirit of Desertion among the Soldiery, never before rose to such a threatening height, as at the present time." On the other hand, he was able to say on February 18 that "There has been no *considerable* desertion from this camp, *to my knowledge within a few days past*" (emphasis added). Even so, writing of the consequences of the lack of clothing, he said that "I am certain Hundreds have deserted" from this cause alone.

Under the articles of war, sentences could take the form of reprimands, fines, or death, without regard to rank. For certain offenses, officers could be cashiered. Enlisted men could be confined, demoted, discharged, or awarded corporal punishment up to 100 lashes. Civilians associated with the army were also subject to the articles. Death was authorized for fourteen offenses, among them being desertion, cowardice, mutiny, and sleeping on guard.

The system had some defects. Washington noted that "There are many little crimes and disorders incident to soldiery, which require immediate punishment and which from the multiplicity of them, if referred to Court Martials, would create endless trouble." Another weakness, he said, was that "the interval between a hundred lashes and death is too great. . . . To inflict a capital punishment upon every deserter or other heinous offender, would incur the imputation of cruelty, and by the familiarity of the example, destroy its efficacy; on the other hand to give only a hundred lashes to such criminals is a burlesque on their crimes." Hence, "whipping should be . . . by no means limited lower than five hundred [lashes]."

At Valley Forge, five soldiers and two civilians were awarded death sentences: in January, two soldiers were hanged for desertion, and in February, a civilian was sentenced to death for acting as a guide for enemy troops. Between early April and the first part of May, three more soldiers were sentenced to death for desertion, but Washington seized the occasion of the May 6 celebration of the alliance with France to pardon them.

The final instance of capital punishment involved Thomas Shanks, an ensign in the 10th Pennsylvania until he was cashiered, during the autumn of 1777, for theft. Embittered, he offered to spy for the British, who sent him to Valley Forge, detailing a sergeant to escort him through the Philadelphia defenses. But the sergeant seized the opportunity to desert; sending Shanks on his way, he took a short cut and was waiting with an alerted provost when Shanks reached the American camp. Shanks was tried on June 2 and hanged on June 4.

In three recorded cases, special steps were taken to humiliate convicted offenders. A commissary, found guilty of stealing $200, was mounted backwards on an unsaddled horse, wearing his coat inside out, his hands tied behind him, and drummed out of the army. A lieutenant convicted of perjury and attempted sodomy and sentenced to be dismissed "with Infamy" was drummed out of camp by all the drummers and fifers of the army, also wearing his coat turned inside out. Perhaps the most bizarre punishment was imposed on another lieutenant, who was "unanimously sentenced to have his sword broke over his head on the grand parade at guard mounting"; further, the court far exceeded normal procedure, stating that after this "just, though mild punishment," it would be "esteem'd a crime of the blackest Dye, in any officer or even soldier to associate with him." According to the record, he had been absent without leave, associating with an enlisted man, and "robbing and infamously stealing." Similar cases brought dishonorable discharges, but without the extra features. The unrecorded details of his crimes must have been exceptionally offensive.

Forty other officers were dismissed, ranging in rank from ensign to lieutenant colonel. However, four of them—all junior officers—were reinstated. Most dismissals were for "conduct unbecoming the character of a gentleman," covering a multitude of sins from being drunk and disorderly to refusal of duty. Theft, misappropriation, and fraud were also fairly common, the most striking of these involving Lieutenant Colonel Neigal Gray, 12th Pennsylvania, who charged his men fees to supplement their rations, then defrauded them of the money they paid.

Courts martial were not always sticklers for regulations. A sergeant wounded a man with his sword, but was let off with a reprimand because of "some alleviating circumstances." A private threatened a lieutenant with a loaded musket, but the "extreme and unpardonable warmth" shown by the lieutenant "renders the actions of the Prisoner in some measure excusable," so the court awarded only a reprimand. A forage-master was tried for abusing and threatening to kill a soldier;

although the court found him guilty, it also stated that "the nature of the insult received by him rendered immediate Chastisement necessary," and did not even bother to hand down a sentence.

A surprising degree of leniency marked the handling of a charge of mutiny and desertion involving an apparent plot between ten soldiers and the wives of two of them, Mary Johnson and Ann McIntire. The court acquitted Ann McIntire, her husband, William, and one other soldier, but convicted the others. One was sentenced merely to a reprimand, and the others to 100 lashes each, with Mary Johnson also to be drummed out of camp. But only Mary Johnson and one soldier were flogged, as the lashes were remitted for the others.

The maximum of 100 lashes, normally specified to be "on the bare back, well laid on," was the usual punishment for desertion. All told, twenty-three soldiers received such sentences, but the floggings were remitted in seven cases. Of the sixteen sentences which were carried out, one was for stealing money, one for plundering, and one for striking a lieutenant; all the rest involved desertion.

For multiple offenses including desertion, two men were sentenced to 500 lashes, two others to 300, and another two to 200, administered fifty at a time. Although for one of these, Washington ordered that the man's back was to be well washed with salt water after the flogging, in all cases except one he held that the sentences were illegal and reduced them to 100 lashes. The one exception was a sentence of 200 lashes for desertion and attempting to escape to the enemy, which was allowed to stand.

Lesser numbers of lashes were also imposed: a private received sixty for threatening the lives of his officers; a sergeant was reduced to private and given fifty lashes for insulting language to three officers, trying to hit a lieutenant with a ramrod, and inciting troops to mutiny; another private, convicted of swearing allegiance to George III, got fifty lashes. A drummer boy was awarded fifty lashes for attempting to desert to the enemy—he was given a reduced sentence "on account of his youth." But a conviction of a soldier on May 3 for desertion brought only thirty-nine lashes; and another soldier was sentenced to a mere twenty-five, but his sole crime was "repeatedly getting drunk."

When drunkenness brought on other offenses, it was still viewed with some tolerance. Private William Harris, 9th Pennsylvania, got drunk and quarrelsome, knocked down a man named Cameron, and threatened to kill him. Private Dennis Kennedy joined in, also striking and abusing Cameron. Further, Kennedy said that he was going to desert just as soon as he could get some shoes, and while he was at it, he cursed Congress. When Harris and Kennedy were taken into custody, Harris lashed out and struck the Corporal of the Guard. Kennedy was sentenced to 100 lashes; but Harris, presumably because he was in his cups, or perhaps because none of his offenses was considered as reprehensible as cursing Congress, got only thirty.

Punishments for civilians caught attempting to assist the enemy were severe. Three men were sentenced to 250 lashes and two others to 200. For three of these floggings, Washington directed a surgeon to be in attendance "to see that the Criminals do not receive more lashes than their strength will bear." Rather surprisingly, a civilian convicted of supplying the enemy with money, trading with them, and dealing in counterfeit Continental currency was sentenced to only 100 lashes, but he was also to be imprisoned for the duration of the war. Three other civilians were sentenced to 100 lashes, but for two of these, Washington commuted the sentences to one month's "constant fatigue." Two others were sentenced to fifty lashes (again, Washington remitted the stripes) and to perform hard labor while the British remained in Pennsylvania unless they chose to enlist in a Continental regiment.

Other punishments of civilians aiding the enemy took the form of fines of £50 or £100—the money being used to benefit the sick—or imprisonment.

Offenses at Valley Forge were what might be expected, considering the semi-trained and half-disciplined character of the army, the pressures of the situation, and the efforts of authority to instil some standards of professional behavior, particularly among the officers. The incidence of courts martial was therefore not unreasonable, especially in view of the lack of other means of handling offenses. Many of the penalties seem barbaric, but they were consistent with eighteenth-century views of punishment under ordinary law. In terms of existing military law, especially as compared with normal Prussian and British practices, they were relatively mild.

Enlisted Men at Valley Forge

All the existing states but Delaware, South Carolina, and Georgia supplied infantry regiments at Valley Forge. There were also five unnumbered regiments, the artillery brigade, and the corps of artificers. In essence, therefore, there was undoubtedly a comprehensive regional representation of the country.

There was also some ethnic diversity. While most troops were of British extraction, some New England regiments in particular included Indian and Negro soldiers. The surgeon of the 1st Connecticut, Dr. Waldo, reported the death of an Indian soldier, presumably in the same regiment, and probably there were other Indians in the ranks. Eventually, there was also a separate unit of Oneida Indians. As for Negroes, during the fall a Hessian officer observed that "One sees no [American] regiment in which there are not Negroes in abundance," and a record of August 24, 1778, shows that in seven brigades there were 378 Negro soldiers. Even if these brigades were at full strength, this figure would still reflect a proportion of Negro soldiers of something over two per cent. Of course, regional differences were significant; and although seven brigades represented nearly half of Washington's infantry, that percentage would probably not apply across the board.

One Negro soldier of a Massachusetts regiment at Valley Forge was Salem Poor, a veteran of Bunker Hill. Apparently, significant elements of the Rhode Island regiments comprising General James Varnum's brigade were Negroes; and on January 2, Varnum proposed enlistment of a special battalion of Rhode Island Negroes. John Laurens twice suggested to his father, Henry Laurens, president of Congress (who proved unreceptive), enlistment of up to five thousand slaves, who would be granted their freedom in return.

The bulk of the army, although of European stock, was not necessarily American-born. The emphasis on assigning only native-born Americans to Washington's Life Guard suggests substantial numbers of immigrants in the ranks. Indeed, foreign-born men in the army were sufficiently numerous to be noticeable in health patterns. Dr. Benjamin Rush reported that "The native Americans were more sickly than the natives of Europe . . . in the American Army."

The American soldier, in theory, was the world's most highly paid enlisted man. New pay rates were announced on May 27, 1778. For infantrymen, monthly pay ranged from $6 2/3 for a private to $10 for a sergeant. The other branches fared better. At one extreme, cannoneers and dragoon privates drew $8 1/3; at the other, cavalry sergeants received $15. In practice, inflation robbed money of its value. In any case, the pay was usually long in arrears.

On January 3, it was announced that Congress had resolved that officers and men continuing in the service would receive an extra month's pay. But the resolution was ambiguous, threatening to sow "great disgust and uneasiness" in the army. Washington said rather testily that "For my part, . . . from the difficulties attending the execution [of the resolutions], I wish they had never been made." In any case, no money was paid until March 11.

The regular pay situation was also bad. On February 3, the average soldier's pay was three months in arrears, with many men having gone unpaid for over five months. A week later, the troops received pay due through the previous November, and December and January pay was issued in late February. But not until the first week of June were the troops paid for February and March.

This was no trifling matter. Washington patiently explained that "Besides feeding and cloathing a soldier well, nothing is of greater importance than paying him with punctuality; and it is perhaps more essential in our army than in any other, because our Men are worse supplied and more necessitous; and the notions of implicit subordination, not being as yet, sufficiently ingrafted among them, they are more apt to reason upon their rights and readier to manifest their sensibility of any thing, that has the appearance of injustice to them; in which light they consider their being kept out of their pay, after it is due."

Certainly, the men had ample incentive to rebel, and Washington seriously anticipated mutiny. Writing on December 23, apparently referring to the chant of "No meat, no meat" on December 21, he said that "I was . . . convinced, that . . . a dangerous Mutiny begun the Night before . . . was still much to be apprehended." Again, on February 14, he asserted that "The Soldiers have been with great difficulty prevented from Mutiny for want of Victuals." Two days later, he stated that "Strong symptoms . . . of discontent have appeared."

As events proved, the bulk of the soldiers were more dedicated than many of their superiors appreciated. Some surliness continued, but no basic erosion of discipline occurred. Captain Duponceau wrote of events in March that "I remember seeing the soldiers . . . calling out in an undertone, 'No bread, no soldier!' " And as late as March 20, Washington said that "Notwithstanding and contrary to my expectations we have been able to keep the Soldiers from Mutiny or dispersion."

The requirements of survival kept the men too occupied to cause trouble. Besides erecting huts, constructing the bridge and fortifications, cutting and hauling firewood, and seeing (admittedly, not too energetically) to the police of the camp area, there were formations to be stood, tours manning pickets and guard posts, and occasional forays against roving British detachments. There was also, particularly after Steuben arrived, an intensive schedule of drill, the drums beating reveille at dawn.

But the Valley Forge soldier's life was not exclusively one of fatigues, deprivations, and the noise of drums. Soon after the army went into winter quarters, Washington issued instructions to regimental commanders. "Let Vice and immorality of every kind be discouraged," he directed, "and see . . . that the Men regularly attend divine Worship. . . . Games of exercise, for amusement, may not only be allowed of, but Incouraged."

During the winter, religious activity was limited by the lack of buildings large enough for services and the lack of clothes to permit the men to endure protracted inactivity listening to sermons outdoors. However, on May 2, orders prescribed services every Sunday; troops whose organizations had no chaplains were to "attend the places of worship nearest them." Washington went on to exhort the army that "To the distinguished Character of Patriot, it should be our highest Glory to add the more distinguished Character of Christian." He also prohibited any Sunday fatigues.

As for "games of exercise, for amusement," during the winter the men probably had neither inclination nor energy for athletics. With warmer weather, however, there were various games—a form of bowling with cannon balls, called "long bullets"; "base," which was probably a version of rounders, the ancestor of baseball; and cricket. Occasionally, there was a rude practical joke, as when "Some Rogueish chaps" tied straw to the tail of a horse, set it afire, and turned the terrified beast loose to run. Understandably, this "very much offended" the horse's owner, who made formal complaint. There is no record, however, of the men responsible being brought to book.

Of what might be called "social life," the enlisted men had almost none. Contact with local families was precluded by restrictions on movement outside camp. During the autumn, a number of women had accompanied the army, but most probably had left by the time the troops reached Valley Forge, although some continued to be a problem.

On February 4, Washington observed that "the most pernicious consequences" had arisen "from suffering persons, women in particular to pass and repass from Philadelphia to camp under Pretence of coming out to visit their Friends in the Army . . . , but really . . . to intice the soldiers to desert." Perhaps this stemmed from the experience with Mary Johnson and Ann McIntire, whose case had been dealt with less than a week earlier.

A few other references exist to women with the troops at Valley Forge. There was mention on March 6 of a soldier's wife selling liquor without permission. On April 26, Dr. Waldo ungallantly observed that

> What! though there are, in rags, in crape, some beings
> here in female shape,
> In whom may still be found some traces of former beauty
> in their faces,
> Yet now so far from being nice, they boast of every
> barefaced vice.
> Shame to their sex! 'Tis not in these one e'er beholds
> those charms that please.

As stated earlier, Washington sought in late May to employ "Women of the Army" as nurses, and in the same order directed that "no Women be suffered on any Pretence to get into the Waggons of the Army on the march." Trial records of June 2 and June 8 mention "Women of bad reputation" in the hut of Sergeant Thomas Howcroft, 10th Pennsylvania, on May 15, and also refer to the presence of the sergeant's family.

From these dates, many of the women apparently came or returned to Valley Forge only when spring arrived. Others, however, evidently endured the winter with the troops. Mrs. Mary Geyer, a laundress on the rolls of the 13th Pennsylvania, accompanied her husband, Peter, and her eleven-year-old son, John, when they enlisted for twenty-one months in the spring of 1776. Peter, a rifleman, and John, a drummer, were wounded at Germantown—Peter being permanently disabled—but all three remained with the army until their enlistments were completed on January 1, 1778. Mary, with John helping, stayed on, continuing to work as a laundress. Another army laundress was a Mrs. Milliner, who remained at Valley Forge to care for her son, Alexander, a drummer boy.

In general, regarding the men in the ranks at Valley Forge, available information tends to concentrate only on such matters as drill schedules, fatigue details, records of punishments, and recitations of shortages. Yet the men's spirits remained remarkably high. The central thrust of all recorded observations is amazement and admiration at the patience, endurance, and fidelity of the troops. In sum, it is clear that one of the most striking characteristics of the American soldier at Valley Forge was that he was a dedicated man, aware of the issues at stake, determined to uphold them, and unshakably confident of the final outcome.

The Officers

In many ways, the officers were worse off than the men. Whereas a soldier was at least theoretically entitled to rations, clothing, and equipment, officers had to follow the European custom of providing their own needs. But while European governments took this into account in establishing pay, Congress did not; and, adopting the concept of "levelling" to eliminate distinctions of status, had authorized pay rates providing marginal differences from one rank to the next. Thus, while the American soldier's prescribed pay—entirely apart from enlistment bounties—was substantially higher than that of the Englishman or Hessian he fought, the American officer drew about a third as much as his British opposite number; and even when officers' pay and allowances were increased by a third on May 27, 1778, the American was still receiving only about half what was paid a British officer of the same rank.

The failure to pay on schedule and the depreciation of money thus hit officers especially hard. Further, the characteristics of maturity and civilian standing which caused individuals to be commissioned in the first place meant that they were especially likely to have heavy responsibilities at home.

Writing on December 28, Dr. Waldo said of officers that "Their Wages will not by considerable, purchase a few Comfortables here in Camp, & maintain their families at home. . . . What then have they to purchase Cloaths and other necessities with?" Continuing, he said that

> . . . Many . . . who depend entirely on their Money [military pay], cannot procure half the material comforts that are wanted in a family. This produces continual letters of complaint from home. When the Officer . . . finds a letter . . . from his Wife, fill'd with the most heart aching tender Complaints, a Woman is capable of writing . . . who would not be disheartened from persevering in the best of Causes. . . ?

Although Washington himself drew no salary, being paid only for his expenses, he was deeply sympathetic. On January 29, he recommended that Congress grant ex-officers after the war half pay for life. This proposition met strong congressional opposition. Repeatedly, Washington emphasized the need. Good officers by the score were resigning. Those who remained, he wrote on April 10, were growing increasingly indifferent to their responsibilities, and cited the number of officers cashiered for dereliction of duty, a trend he said would continue "Untill Officers consider their Commissions in an honorable, and [materially] interested point of view, and are afraid to endanger them by negligence or inattention." Nevertheless, not until May 18 was congressional approval of a half-pay measure announced. Even then, opponents blocked full adoption. What was provided was that officers remaining in the service for the duration of the war would receive half pay for seven years thereafter, or until the officer died, whichever occurred sooner.

New monthly pay scales were established on May 27. Artillerymen drew the highest salaries, ranging from $100 for a colonel to $33 1/3 for a second lieutenant. An infantry colonel got $75, and an ensign $20. Cavalry pay, due to the extra costs of maintaining mounts, ran from the $93 3/4 of a colonel to the $26 2/3 of a cornet. In addition, on June 3 officers were granted a monthly ration allowance, beginning at $10 and increasing in $10 increments by grade to the colonel's $50.

But when the army first reached Valley Forge, all this was months in the future. It is small wonder, therefore, that there was an immediate landslide of leave applications. On December 22, Washington had to rule that he himself would approve all leaves for captains and above. But the problem continued. On February 9, he was writing that "It is a matter of no small grief to me, to find such an unconquerable desire in the Officers of this Army to be absent."

This by no means applied merely to junior officers. On December 27, Washington refused permission for Anthony Wayne to leave camp until the huts were built; as of January 9, he was urging Generals Learned and Glover to return from leave; General Muhlenberg was on leave in February, and Generals Woodford and Scott had made application. At one time in February there were only three major generals in camp, several brigades were without brigadiers, and many regiments had no officers present above the rank of captain. Understandably, Washington felt obliged to refuse applications from Generals Sullivan and Varnum. This last, however, was couched in such courtly language that Varnum could hardly have felt resentment, as Washington concluded with the hope that "you will . . . endeavour to conciliate your happiness with the public Interest and the good of the Service."

Not all requests were rejected as graciously. Colonel William Malcom, who had relatively little service, was told that "You cannot be surprised that I disapproved your application." Washington went on to say that "However anxious I might have been before for your continuance in the Army, . . . if you can obtain liberty from Congress to resign, . . . you will meet with no difficulty with me."

Resignations, indeed, were legion. On December 28, Dr. Waldo claimed that "Yesterday upwards of fifty Officers in Gen¹ Greene's Division resigned. . . . Six or Seven of our Regiment are doing the like today." By February 18, Washington was saying that "The spirit of resigning, which is now become almost epidemical, is truely painful and alarming."

Officer morale was also depressed by the lack of any clear or equitable system of appointment and promotion.

Congress had been lavish in bestowing military rank on commissaries and others who, although performing important tasks, were not officers of the army. Noting this, Washington wrote that "No error can be more pernicious than that of dealing out rank with too prodigal a hand." When a vacancy occurred within a regiment, it was often claimed by such officers. Predictably, regimental officers thought that vacancies should be filled from among themselves. Such cases had caused "uneasiness, discord and perplexity," resulting in "numerous bickerings and resignations," and "occasioned infinite trouble and vexation."

The lack of established regulations, the different sources of appointment, and the complications injected because some officers had not served continuously brought on serious disputes over seniority. One such dispute involved no less than four brigadiers, two of whom threatened to leave the service. With difficulty, Washington persuaded one of the disgruntled generals to relent, but he failed completely with the other.

In a similar case, a protest by captains of the Pennsylvania Line required a board to convene on February 16 to rule on the competing claims to the position of major, 10th Pennsylvania. Another controversy concerned a French volunteer, Chevalier du Plessis, who claimed position in the artillery brigade according to his brevet (honorary) rank of lieutenant colonel. The resentful artillery officers formed a committee to protest; Washington repeatedly contended that brevet rank did not affect seniority, but the committee as often maintained that it did, and the matter was settled only when Du Plessis resigned. Still another dispute arose when Major John Popkins, 3d Artillery, was promoted to lieutenant colonel in his own regiment although Major Thomas Forrest, 4th Artillery, was senior. Promotion was by seniority within a regiment, but the question was taken up by the artillery officers' committee.

Truly, as Dr. Waldo observed, "Rank & Precedence make a good deal of disturbance & confusion in the American Army." However, it would be wrong to blame these controversies on pettiness. To a degree, of course, they reflected offended vanity. More fundamentally, however, they were caused by the lack of any clear-cut appointment and promotion system. (In desperation, Washington wrote on May 29 that "My earnest wish is that something, I do not care what, may be fixed and the regulations compleated. . . .") And in one sense, they were a healthy sign that since at least some of the officers valued their commissions, the army was moving—however slowly—toward a point where Washington's misgivings about deterioration of quality through indifference would become unjustified.

But officers at Valley Forge were not preoccupied exclusively with bickering. They had routine duty as officers of the day, at guard mount, on picket, and taking part in frequent patrolling. Clearly, they must have spent a great deal of time serving on courts martial. After Steuben's training program began, they were increasingly involved in detailed supervision of the troops. There was also the matter of improving their own knowledge. At the outset, Washington pointed out that "As War is a science, . . . a great deal of useful knowledge and Instruction [is] to be drawn from Books," and told the regimental commanders that "you are to cause your Officers to devote some part of their time to reading Military Authors." How faithfully this directive was observed may be questioned. Certainly there were instances of ineptitude, and on March 26, a General Order prohibited unauthorized scouting parties, as "Many officers have been captivated by their own folly and carelessness."

The lieutenants and ensigns in particular fully shared the men's hardships and deprivations and, as Captain Duponceau noted, demonstrated similar dedication and endurance. They also shared the hazards of disease and exposure. Sufficient numbers died for funerals to become a problem, and a General Order of April 12 directed that "The Funeral Honors at the Interment of Officers are . . . to be confined to a solemn Procession . . . suitable to the rank of the deceased . . . ; Firing [of salutes] on those occasions . . . is to be abolished."

There were attempts to provide amenities. Of the 13th Pennsylvania, for example, Lieutenant James McMichael reported that on January 14,

> At the request of Colonel [Walter] Stewart, the officers of the regiment were summoned to dine with him, where we spent the day in civil jolity. In this manner several days were spent, passing by a rotation from the senior to the junior officers. . . . While confined to camp, we passed many hours in recreation, viewing the environs thereof. . . .

37

But "viewing the environs" was not merely for amusement, for Mc-Michael comments that the officers "surveyed the most advantageous posts in case of an attack."

The custom whereby the field and general officers of the day dined with Washington constituted another social activity. A change had to be made, however, when it was found that this practice hampered them in making their rounds; thereafter, the officers of the day dined with Washington on the day following their duty tours.

Another pastime was instituted early in February. "Some gentlemen of the camp Hospital being desirous of improving in the accomplishment of dancing," it was announced, "Mr. John Trotter has agreed to open a school for their accommodation." Mr. Trotter, with long experience as a dancing master in New York, was "about" fifty-eight years old; but "the ease and grace with which he moves on the floor, evince, that . . . he has lost none of his agility by age."

In January, General Greene's wife, Catherine, arrived at Valley Forge. Martha Washington reached camp by February 10. Elias Boudinot, the commissioner for exchange of prisoners, noted that she was "almost a mope for want of a female companion" and sent for his wife to keep her company. General Lord Stirling's wife and daughter were also in camp, as was Rebecca Biddle, whose husband was Colonel Clement Biddle, the forage-master general. Lucy Knox, wife of General Henry Knox, did not arrive until May 20; Mrs. Greene, on the other hand, started home about May 25, and Mrs. Washington left on June 9. Probably some of the other officers also brought their wives to Valley Forge. General De Kalb speaks of fifteen hundred officers and ladies attending the celebration of the French alliance on May 6, and while the ladies would have been greatly outnumbered, the statement implies far more than the seven who have been mentioned.

Mrs. Greene lived for a time in a hut, and Alexander Milliner reported that Martha Washington pinned her clothes with thorns. But the women added an element of civility. Probably they prompted a number of relatively elaborate entertainments. On April 15, for example, some officers and ladies staged a play for an audience jamming the "Bakehouse," and on May 11, Joseph Addison's play, *Cato*, was presented.

As for more active recreations, when spring came the officers played "base" and "wicket" (cricket). Indeed, one day early in May, after dining with General Knox, Washington himself took a bat to join a cricket match with the artillery officers.

For officers and men, Valley Forge was a time of training, but for officers it was also a time of weeding out. Numerous dismissals went far to remove those who were deficient in character or ability; resignations eliminated many who lacked determination, or who had to give first priority to family claims; the half-pay measure provided a material incentive; and Steuben's example and instruction opened new horizons regarding the scope of officers' duties. Those remaining, therefore, were well on the way to becoming the nucleus of the corps of dedicated, proficient, and responsible leaders whose role was to be crucial to the ultimate success of the war.

WASHINGTON AT VALLEY FORGE

At Valley Forge, Washington was personally involved in every aspect of the army's existence, from broad policy to the most minute details. There was no one able or available to help him significantly. Even such a rudimentary staff as was then understood was essentially lacking, and Washington's "staff" actually consisted chiefly of aides and military secretaries.

As for his personal situation, the Isaac Potts house was better than

Drawing by H. T. McNeill, courtesy Stephen Moylan Press.

The Isaac Potts House, rented by Washington for his quarters at Valley Forge.

a tent or a hut, but for a considerable period he was inconvenienced by the absence of his personal equipment, which had accompanied the army's baggage in mid-December. As late as January 11, he was trying to have it located and returned. Washington's Negro servant, Billy Lee, saw to the General's personal comfort, and after Martha Washington arrived she undoubtedly relieved her husband of many distracting details. Probably, too, she was behind the celebration of his forty-fifth birthday on February 22, following which the general and his guests were serenaded by the fifers and drummers of the 2d Artillery. He himself did not go out to greet them, but Martha conveyed his thanks and tipped them fifteen shillings.

Washington may have been constrained by diffidence, but this event took place during the worst part of the army's famine, and within days after he had been writing of the danger of mutiny. He may have suspected that what was ostensibly a musical compliment might really be a disguise for a deputation. If so, his action showed prudent restraint.

Yet it is clear that Washington enjoyed the men's confidence, and criticisms from the rest of the population aroused indignation in the army. Dr. Waldo wrote on December 26:

> Why don't his Excellency rush in & retake the City [Philadelphia] . . . ? Because he knows better than to leave his Post and be catch'd like a d————d fool. . . . His conduct when closely scrutinised is uncensurable.

And Washington's standing did not decline. On March 20, Lieutenant McMichael wrote that "We rely on the prudence and skill of our worthy General."

Notwithstanding the diarists' views, Washington's military skill was challenged by many. He had been deceived at Brandywine, outmaneuvered at the Schuylkill, and at Germantown his plan was far too complicated for the state of his troops' training. Indeed, the coalescence of criticism resulted in the so-called "Conway Cabal," aimed at replacing Washington with General Horatio Gates.

Gates, who had served for twenty years as a Regular officer in the British army, had been credited with the major victory at Saratoga in October, 1777. Now, he was at York as president of the Board of War which, under Congress, was roughly analogous to the modern Department of Defense.

Lending his influence was General Thomas Mifflin, a prominent Pennsylvanian. He fancied himself a strategist and disagreed with the priorities Washington felt compelled to accept. Uninterested in his assignment as Quartermaster General, he resigned, but Congress soon named him to the Board of War.

The prime mover, however, was General Thomas Conway. Born in Ireland, he had served twenty-eight years in the French army when he came to America in the spring of 1777. Appointed a brigadier general, he showed considerable ability, but his boastfulness and supercilious attitude toward American officers caused resentment in the army even while his adroit intriguing won him supporters in Congress and brought his promotion to major general and appointment to the key post of Inspector General.

As early as November 8, Washington learned that Conway was plotting with Gates against him. Because there was opposition to Washington by some members of Congress, this situation potentially threatened him, and the problem was compounded by rumors of dissatisfaction which Mifflin spread within the army. On the other hand, Washington had strong congressional support, which increased as the Committee on Conference reported the scale of the problems he faced. Further, Gates made the mistake of trying to dissemble his part, sending Washington a letter which was incompatible with earlier disclaimers and in some respects even internally contradictory, but defending Conway. In a reply of January 23, Washington enumerated Gates's inconsistencies and demolished Conway with biting sarcasm. Gates had overreached himself. Seeing members of Congress reversing their favorable view of Conway, and noting the steadfast support given Washington by such key officials as Henry Laurens, on February 19 Gates wrote Washington a conciliatory letter; and on February 24, Washington agreed somewhat stiffly to drop the issue. Although some weeks later Dr. Benjamin Rush was still circulating a letter attacking Washington's competence, by February 28 Washington was convinced that the affair had blown over. It was laid to rest permanently when, on April 22, Conway resigned.

Through the winter, Washington's morale ranged from near-hopelessness to ebullient optimism. His forebodings concerning the army's chances for mere survival have been noted, as well as his bleak assessments regarding the prospects of mutiny. Even before he had word of the French alliance, though, Washington's mood changed, and on May 2 he spoke of "the signal Instances of providential Goodness" which "have now almost crowned our labours with complete Success."

Washington was too able a leader to reveal any misgivings. But as the situation bettered, there were instances when his self-control slipped briefly, letting his new exuberance show through. In particular, there was the formal celebration of the French alliance when, riding away

41

to his officers' cheers, he turned repeatedly, waving his hat in the air and shouting "Huzza!"

In sum, the achievement of Valley Forge is in many respects due to Washington's personal influence. Whatever his technical limitations as a soldier, his capacity for inspiring his followers' esteem and trust was undeniably a key factor in the army's endurance of its long and agonizing ordeal.

Highlights and Special Events

After the December 21 low point, there was considerable aggressive patrolling. Indeed, on December 22, a detachment was sent on a week's patrol, and a 150-man force went out on January 12. Sometimes there were clashes. The December 22 patrol captured a dozen British dragoons, but lost 18 men. Another engagement occurred on January 18, when Captain Henry Lee and seven of the Light Horse drove off a force of almost two hundred British cavalrymen, guided by local Tories, who surprised their bivouac.

Less dramatic, but of great long-range importance, was the arrival in late January of the "Committee on Conference" which Congress had appointed to work with Washington "for introducing œconomy and promoting discipline and good morals in the army." The members were Francis Dana, Joseph Reed, Nathaniel Folsom, Charles Carroll, Gouverneur Morris, and John Harvie. Holding frequent sessions from January 28 until well into April, they played a key role in making Congress realize the army's dire needs; they helped make it possible for the able Nathanael Greene to be appointed Quartermaster General; and their persuasion was important in congressional adoption of reforms which made significant contributions to preserving the army and establishing a sound basis for its continued operation.

March 17 saw a potentially disturbing episode when some Pennsylvania soldiers made a scarecrow, labeled it "Paddy," and set it up beside the sector of Colonel Daniel Morgan's 11th Virginia, many of whose members were Irishmen. They took deep offense, but mistakenly blamed Massachusetts troops. Morgan's men were as hard-bitten as any in the army; the New Englanders disliked Virginians in any case, and were full of outraged innocence. Noisy threats were exchanged, but Washington—summoned by an apprehensive Officer of the Day—arrived before any actual violence occurred.

A quick check showed that no one knew who was responsible for the offending scarecrow. Demonstrating a clear grasp of soldier psychology, Washington put on a fine display of fury, outdoing even the

Irishmen in his anger. As an admirer of St. Patrick, he would not tolerate such an outrage. As soon as he learned who in fact was responsible, he would make the culprit permanently regretful. Confronted with more support than they had bargained for, and unable to identify who had actually set up the "Paddy," Morgan's men began to feel sheepish—as Washington must have anticipated. To save face all around, he gave orders for a gill of spirits to be issued to each soldier, turning a potentially nasty situation into an impromptu celebration.

May 1 saw an event involving the bulk of the soldiers. The day was the special holiday of a super-patriots' organization called the Society of King Tammany, taking its name from a friendly Indian leader in early Pennsylvania.

The celebration was planned and carried out exclusively by the enlisted men. At reveille, according to Lieutenant George Ewing, "mirth and Jollity" began when soldiers, wearing white blossoms in their hats, followed fifers and drummers, parading past the May poles in each regimental area. The men of the 3d New Jersey then trooped off to Washington's headquarters to cheer the Commander-in-Chief. "But just as they were descending the hill to the house an Aide met them and informed them that the General was indisposed and desired them to retire. . . ."

Although the episode sounds orderly, it must have been feared that the men might become rowdy. In any case, Lieutenant Ewing showed obvious relief in reporting that they marched back to their own sector, cheering at each May pole they passed but observing "the greatest decency and regularity." Then, after "taking a drink of Whiskey which a Generous contribution of their officers had procured for them they dismisd and each man retird to his own hut without any incident hapening throughout the whole day."

A still greater celebration took place on May 6, with "rejoysing throughout the whole Army" in observance of the Treaty of Alliance with France.

Brigades assembled at 9 A.M. for an hour and a half of prayer and "discourse" by their chaplains. At 10:30, on a signal fired from the artillery park, the men fell in for inspection. An hour later, following another cannon shot, the brigades marched to their parade positions, forming two long ranks. Meanwhile, "Thirteen six Pounders were drove to a height in the rear of Conways Brigade." Then Washington trooped the line on horseback, after which he, his aides, and the Life Guard took post on a slight rise to the right rear. At this juncture, the flag on Fort Washington was lowered and a third gun was fired from the artillery park, signaling the fieldpieces on the hill to begin a thirteen-gun salute. As soon as that was completed, a *feu de joie* of musketry rippled down the ranks. Advance instructions specified that at this stage "The whole Army will Huzza! 'Long Live the King of France.'" Then came another thirteen-gun salute from the heights, another *feu de joie*, and a cheer, "Long Live the Friendly European Powers." The same procedure was carried out once more, ending with a cheer "to the American States." The directive concluded that "Each man is to have a Gill of rum." Despite the intricacy of the ceremony, Captain Laurens claimed that "The order with which the whole was conducted, [and] the beautiful effect of the running fire, which was executed to perfection, . . . gave sensible pleasure to everyone present."

Not quite the whole army took part. Morgan's Virginians were patrolling toward Philadelphia—"The enemy may think to take advantage of the celebration of this day," their orders stated, and "the troops must have more than the common quantity of liquor, and perhaps there will be some little drunkenness among them."

A party followed the review. "There was a grand harber [arbor] bilt," noted Elijah Fisher, who was now a member of Washington's Life Guard, "and all the Commissioners [commissioned officers] were Envited to dine with His Exelency." There, Lieutenant Ewing said, they enjoyed a "cold collation . . . where many patriotic Toasts were drank and the [day] concluded with harmless Mirth and jollity." Considering the warmth of emotion, the significance of the occasion, and perhaps the number of toasts, it is hardly surprising that as Washington rode away he split the air with repeated shouts of "Huzza!"

But problems remained. On February 3, Congress had directed Washington to have all officers take oaths of allegiance and abjuration. Noting the temper of his officers, Washington deliberately procrastinated, but by early May they had become more receptive. Accordingly, on May 7 he announced the requirement and established a procedure "in order to carry out this very interesting and essential work." Many officers had reservations, however. On May 11, Washington was urging that the oaths be administered as soon as possible to the officers of the 3d and 4th New Jersey regiments, who had overcome their objections, "as there is some little boggle in this matter in other Corps . . . [and] it will be a good example to others." Apparently, the example worked for all units except Woodford's Virginia brigade, twenty-six of whose officers protested that the oath implied an indignity; it would freeze their existing ranks; it would preclude resignations; and it committed them to accept the unsatisfactory existing establishment.

Patiently, Washington refuted the objections and the officers were duly sworn.

At this time, the most ambitious of the forays from Valley Forge took place. British evacuation of Philadelphia was rumored and Washington decided to send a detachment toward the city, large enough to pursue the British if evacuation was imminent. This task force numbered over two thousand troops, including the recently arrived Oneida Indians and part of the Life Guard. Lafayette was given command.

Crossing the Schuylkill soon after midnight on May 19, the Americans deployed at Barren Hill, about twelve miles from Philadelphia. The river protected the south against a British attack, Light Horse patrols covered the front, and Pennsylvania militia cavalry was supposed to be watching the northern approaches.

Actually, the British knew of the American move, and were planning to capture Lafayette's force. Howe himself would lead a column to attack the front of the American position. General Charles Grey was to lead another column against the American left flank. The third column, under General James Grant, would swing north, well beyond the American line, then cut southeast to get between Barren Hill and the nearest ford to its rear.

The Pennsylvania militia supposedly covering the north had never taken position, and Grant was almost at Barren Hill when someone happened to see his column and hurried to Lafayette with the news. Soon afterwards, the Light Horse captured two British soldiers who said that other forces were on the way. The word that spread at Barren Hill, Elijah Fisher wrote, was that "The howl of Gen. How's Army was Advansing upon us in three Colloms. . . . The Nuse alarmed us Enstantly. . . ."

The only solution was to race Grant's column to Matson's Ford while a rear guard delayed the British advance. The escape was not completed without difficulty, however. Private Fisher reported that, crossing the Schuylkill, "the warter was up to our middle and run very swift so that we were obliged to hold to each other to keep the Corrent from sweeping us away and all in a fluster expecting the Enemy to fire in upon us for we could see them Plain . . . but we got all Safe across . . . save fore or five of our party that the Enemy's Lite horse Cut to pieces and our flanks killed three of there Lite Draghoons and four of there Granadears."

Howe was unwilling to risk attacking across the river and started back to Philadelphia. The Americans bivouacked at Gulph Mills. Next morning, they returned to Barren Hill, remaining until May 23, then marched back to Valley Forge.

Epilogue

From then on, all energies were directed toward preparations for active pursuit of the British as soon as Philadelphia was abandoned, and when word reached Washington just before noon on June 18 that the British had left the city during the night, the Americans were ready to start one division moving before the afternoon was over. The rest of the army followed on June 19, six months to the day after they had come limping in to begin their winter encampment.

There can have been few regrets among the soldiers who stepped out smartly, leaving Valley Forge behind them. But regardless of the misery of the preceding months, the army and the nation just coming into being had gained something of lasting value.

These soldiers were a far cry from the ragged, freezing, half-starved collection of men who had begun the encampment. They had become an army—proficient in the skills of their trade, responsive to their leaders, and for the first time competently and responsibly led. The road ahead was long and full of adversity, but since December the army had taken a giant step toward achievement of the new nation's ultimate goal of firmly established independence.

Thus, the country as a whole had gained a major benefit in terms of its immediate objective. And in a broader sense, it had gained perhaps even more by being provided with an example of dedication and fortitude and sacrifice to which it could look for renewed strength and faith throughout all the decades to come.